Social Media Marketing

A Comprehensive Guide to Growing
Your Brand on Social Media

Table of Contents

Introduction 1

Chapter 1: The Power of Social Media 4

Chapter 2: Understand Today's Social Media Platforms 9

Chapter 3: The Many Roles of Social Media and Content

Marketing 17

Chapter 4: Build Your Brand 25

Chapter 5: Create Quality Content...30

Chapter 6: Craft Your Social Media Strategy...........................38

Chapter 7: Enhance Your Reach and Engagement...................54

Chapter 8: Social Media Marketing Tools 61

Chapter 9: Monitor and Measure Success..............................68

Conclusion...76

Introduction

Not so long ago, social media marketing was still just a concept in development. Platforms like Facebook, Twitter, and Instagram are making it amazingly easy for businesses to convey their message, identity, and products to millions of people, all without having to spend millions of dollars in the process.

Looking at the current marketing landscape, social media is clearly dictating the industry. There is no doubt that social media has seen many developments that have allowed it to become focused on information gathering, making it the best place for a brand to attract its target audience.

Make no mistake; using social media effectively is no easy feat. There are strategists, writers, managers, designers, and many other highly specialized individuals who contribute to the success a social media campaign. This doesn't mean that there isn't a space for you to enter the game; but understanding how the big picture works is essential for your success. Social media companies depend heavily on advertising and marketing to make their profits, giving small businesses a chance to advertise their products and services to the masses.

Social media presence and experience is primordial to maintain a competitive edge in the world of business. This book's goal is to clear the fog surrounding social media metrics, best practices, and the continuous updates that grant advertisers more power and leeway. While the true benefits of social media aren't explicitly tied to their marketing or advertising potential, they also have an impact on product design, efficiency, productivity, and other core business parameters.

Invariably, you'll notice that the most successful brands on social media are those with a story to tell, not to mention an interesting one that can stand out from the competition. The resonance of these brands with consumers is quite effective at driving broad brand recognition and impressions. Niche brands that never had a big enough market to supply to, can finally connect with millions of customers across the globe thanks to the widespread reach of social media. While already established brands have the advantage of consumers seeking them out, smaller businesses can leverage the quick pace and style of social media to make an impact.

Creating content is the essence of any powerful social media campaign, but before you dive into content creation, there are different parameters that you must assess. The audience you're targeting, budget, social media platform, implementation timeframe, and many other metrics you want to make sure you've got right before you embark on that journey. With billions of global users, almost any brand or niche business can find a remarkable market segment without having to spend millions.

Throughout this book, you'll discover the true potential social media markets offer to you as a business and an individual, in addition to understanding the marketing mechanics of the most prominent social media platforms. Content marketing, reach, and brand recognition will also be taken into consideration as you build your brand. Without further ado, now that you've got an idea of what lies ahead, let's dive right in!

Chapter 1: The Power of Social Media

To understand the influence of social media, it's important to explore the origins and foundations that these companies have driven power from. The dynamics that govern social media are quite organic, even if technology did play an important role in propelling their development. Influence is the currency of social media platforms, and by making it more controllable, they have the power to persuade people to consume content, purchase products, and many other concepts that can be powerful in practice.

The Emergence of Social Media

The business sphere, where advertising and marketing dominate a big sector, has been overtaken by social media, not to mention its influence on education. If you look closely, you'll notice that the impact social media has on such industries derives from communication. The ways in which we communicate have changed with the rise of social media platforms. For example, WhatsApp became the new definition of instant messaging, removing traditional SMS texts from most equations. Aside from the device, an internet connection is all you need to reach anyone anywhere on the globe. Social media's impact on communication standards has always been a topic of great interest and discussion among influential tables, public and private alike.

The reason online communication is so powerful is its capacity to bring information to light, especially information that would've been impossible to access using conventional methods. The advancement in awareness in today's generation can mainly be credited to the influence of social media and the hyper-paced nature of information technology. Knowing what's happening around you in the world may have been a dire task in the past, but nowadays, all you need is internet access and a social media account. A single impactful event can spread like wildfire through everyone's newsfeed, thanks to the power of sharing. In parallel, advertisements and products are being showered on individuals who happen to be interested. Thanks to the algorithms used to target certain population segments, many influential entities, from movements to commercial services, rely on social media to relay their message to the masses.

Impact on Business Strategies

When everything is a few clicks away, options become infinite, making it essential for businesses to compete within specific markets. This ease of access to information is a formidable tool that can be used by businesses to find and reach their customers. The conventional methods of shopping in grocery stores or reading newspapers have been overhauled by this new digital landscape. Even students utilize social media to create chat rooms where they can interact and share files conveniently. The local boundaries that restricted many businesses have been removed thanks to the far-reaching powers of the internet. Digital marketing through social platforms is no longer a new fad, but rather a central tool that can dictate entire business strategies.

The Nature of Online Payments

E-payments now allow a lot of digital services to widen their scope, thanks to the effortless nature of online monetary transactions. Even though online banking services were the first effectively proven form of online payment, social platforms are carving themselves a piece of the pie; WhatsApp for example, is experimenting with a new payment system that enables users to exchange money easily. While these payment systems are quite efficient, there are challenges posed by security standards and their maintenance.

Impact on Healthcare

Perhaps surprisingly, the healthcare industry has seen positive reinforcement from the integration of social media into its infrastructure. The classic method of visiting a doctor to diagnose an ailment is slowly being replaced by virtual health practitioners who will analyze your symptoms. While the virtual way may not yet be as efficient as physical consultations, it is helpful in times where visiting the doctor may carry a risk. The COVID-19 pandemic has prompted many people to resort to virtual doctors to avoid risking infection, not to mention that some hospitals encourage virtual consultations for diagnosis. This type of healthcare allows people to digitally cross the borders of their country and visit with globally recognized doctors for assessment and treatment.

The Improvement of Civic Awareness

The large scale of civic movements that have emerged in the era of social media is quite astounding when compared to the age of printed media. The reason a lot of people are becoming more aware of the issues that trouble the world is the speed and fluidity of information exchange between individuals. Social platforms have given voice to almost everyone, which naturally means that a lot of concerns that may have previously been entirely restricted to local geography have suddenly become global matters. From natural catastrophes to political corruption, people's civic awareness is now drawn from digital sources rather than governments and conventional media sources.

Transform Brands into Humans

Businesses were always viewed as cold entities devoid of human emotions. Nevertheless, social platforms have slowly nudged businesses into warmer waters, creating human-like brands that interact with their customers and followers. The last few years have seen a rising trend in the "humanification" of businesses. This trend was expected as the voices of the masses have become ubiquitous through reviews, comments, or shares. The word goes around, and when the audience comprises millions of people, brands have to pay attention to the microenvironment and make changes to their macro strategies. People trust people more than names and rigid commercial entities, which made businesses pivot to becoming 'warmer,' replying to comments and coming up with transparent communication strategies.

The Power of Reach

'Reach' is a term often used in the context of social media's influence on people. Having a high reach simply means connecting with more people. Although a business isn't necessarily a numbers game, reaching more people will invariably translate into more sales. Whether it's a private venture or an NGO, acquiring reach is primordial for the organization if it wants to be heard. Within different contexts, organizations view reach as a tool to reach various goals, from improving brand image to attracting more customers.

Chapter 2: Understand Today's Social Media Platforms

Choosing the right social media platform is crucial, as it can make or break your marketing strategy. Since every website offers different interfaces, features, and audiences, it is necessary to scrutinize each platform to make an informed choice.

The following social media platforms are extremely popular nowadays and hold massive potential for promoting your business. Let's look at each platform and understand its potential to create brand awareness and engagement.

Facebook

With over 2 billion monthly users, Facebook is the world's largest social media platform. It attracts 74% of American users on a daily basis. Despite many uninformed brands thinking that the platform only caters to baby boomers, Facebook attracts 51% of teenagers and 79% of young adult demographics.

How it helps: Facebook allows you to post all forms of content, including images, text, videos, stories, and live streams. This gives you flexibility and the ability to experiment with different

9

forms of content. Unless you do not have a designated content plan, you can use Facebook to test out your strategy. One of the platform's highlights is the ability to create private groups and take advantage of its dedicated online communities. If done right, your brand can attract several potential customers at once. It is also useful for e-commerce integration and running ads. Newer updates allow users to interact with the brand of their choice and shop directly on their Facebook page. The platform's algorithm also targets users who share your brand's values and who may enjoy your products or services.

Instagram

Thanks to its rising popularity, Instagram should not be left out. With over 1 billion global users, this platform has boomed over the past 5 years and is gaining more traction. Even though it is now owned by Facebook, Instagram has maintained its own identity and stands out from others.

How it helps: Instagram is, by far, the most popular choice for upcoming and existing brands. This platform's interface compels you to post unique, visually appealing content. Not unlike Facebook, Instagram offers a myriad of options to post various forms of content. You can publish still images, videos, GIFs, stories, live videos, Q&As, polls, and more. The newest most popular feature introduced in 2020 is Reels, which displays 15 to

30-second clips covering the entire screen. Brands and content creators alike have applauded this new feature. If your brand caters to a younger audience, Instagram is certainly the right choice for you.

Snapchat

This social media platform was once one of the top sites for engagement. Today, it still attracts users with its new and exciting features launched but isn't the same powerhouse it once was. On the application, you click photos and send them as 'Snaps' to your friends on your list, which last for 24 hours. You can also use filters, added effects, augmented reality (AR), music, and other unique features on your snaps. With on demand geo-filters, users can add a custom filter to their snaps at a relatively cheap cost.

How it helps: While Snapchat can be an odd choice for brands, it is highly effective to create interaction among users of the same age group. It is one of the best platforms to target the Gen Z population, as it attracts 73% of teenagers and 47% of young adults. If your brand offers products or services for users between the ages of 12 and 24, Snapchat deserves a top spot on your list. You can also generate user engagement by developing custom filters or holding contests and giveaways.

Twitter

This highly interactive social media platform attracts over 330 million users globally. It allows you to 'tweet' captions, headlines, and random thoughts in a text format not exceeding 280 characters. Since most users have a short attention span, tweets garner maximum attention, and spread worthy information in a creative and concise manner. Twitter also enables you to post images and videos, yet it majorly thrives on text posts.

How it helps: If you want to keep things simple and to the point, Twitter is your go-to platform. Its character limit and straightforward approach encourage brands to get as creative as possible. Recently, Twitter has been witnessing funny feuds and witty comebacks from brands as a marketing strategy. While most of them are part of a promotional act, some brands are applauded for their responsiveness and humor. Since this platform mainly attracts teenagers and young adults, it can be leveraged to promote brands that target these audiences. The use of hashtags and digital ads are other valuable highlights; Twitter lets you tailor your digital and social media marketing strategy with its versatile ad format options.

YouTube

As the world's largest platform to consume video content, YouTube attracts around 1.9 billion users, of which 85 to 90%

are aged 13 to 49. In terms of usage, it competes with Facebook and Instagram, which are already quite popular among social media users. YouTube is also recognized as the second largest search engine after Google, giving you an opportunity to target your audience and reach millions of users at once.

How it helps: Most social media users prefer video content as it presents and explains things in a fun, digestible, and entertaining way. If your social media strategy revolves around using visuals to promote your products and services, YouTube is your answer. Shoot product videos, 'how to use' clips, tutorials, interviews, and behind-the-scenes videos. Although YouTube marketing is effective, it requires a lot of time and effort to build a name for your brand on this platform, given its competitiveness. An appreciable highlight is the use of SEO (search engine optimization), which allows you to use specific keywords in your titles and videos to strengthen the search results and improve your rankings.

TikTok

In early 2018, TikTok grew massively and was one of the most downloaded apps worldwide. The platform promotes a video content form that enables users to upload music videos showcasing their talent for dancing, lip singing, and more. It also provides a ton of filters, effects, and music options to make posts more interesting and entertaining. Since videos cover the entire phone screen, the interface is well-received by users.

How it helps: If you prefer to put out your message in a light and breezy way, TikTok is an ideal choice. The 60-second video content format is easy to digest and can reach millions of users, but it doesn't attract users of all ages and interests, which can be quite limiting. Despite being banned in a few countries, TikTok is still surging in popularity. Brands often use it to upload lively video content such as 'how-to' clips, behind-the-scenes, or time-lapse videos.

Reddit

Reddit can be considered a niche within the world of social media. Even though it caters to a specific audience, the platform lets you build an organic community, which can be highly beneficial for your brand. Reddit receives over 2 billion page views every month, and its content marketing potential is incredible. Users can submit questions, reply to threads, post images and links, and vote on them. Dedicated forums, also known as subreddits, help target user groups and enhance user engagement.

How it helps: If you want to learn more about your audience and not just attract more potential customers, Reddit is your go-to platform. You can delve deeper and understand your users' thoughts, interests, or responses to current trends, which is useful for improving your products and customer experience. When it comes to marketing your brand on Reddit, you need to be extra careful, as users can cross-question and berate your content. Do not post content that is overly promotional or feels spam-y. To avoid losing credibility, make sure your content will be received by the tech-savvy, liberal, and 'geeky' community. If you are successful, you can build your brand and achieve tremendous success in record time.

Which Platform is the Best for Your Brand?

Ultimately, your social media strategy may be effective, but it will not work if you target the wrong platform. Choose a platform that welcomes your target audience, which can be decided by studying your ideal customer and understanding their needs. The platform you select should also align with the type of content you create. Most audio, video, and text-based content are recognized as macro content. By contrast, bite-sized content and posts comprise micro-content and are easy to digest by most online users. Lastly, only pick two to three social media platforms and master the art of using these channels to convey your brand's values and build its image.

Since posting regularly and maintaining social media pages is not an easy task, stick to just two or three platforms and focus on delivering quality content as much as possible. Apart from these popular social media platforms used today, LinkedIn, Pinterest, and Quora are also used by some brands. If you wish to promote your business on a B2B basis, LinkedIn is the right choice for you.

Chapter 3: The Many Roles of Social Media and Content Marketing

It's hard to deny the impact social media has had on all kinds of professional endeavors. Naturally, any money-making platform comes with its own unique roles. Social media platforms are considered a wide spectrum, branching out across various marketing maneuvers and strategies to allow brands to boost engagement and drive sales. If you want to work in such a field, it's important to get familiar with the different roles required in the creation of social media marketing content.

The Evolution of Career Options

Digital marketing has experienced a serious bump ever since the introduction of social media in the late 2000s. As platforms evolve, so do skills, career options, and certifications. The professional standards and licenses of working in social media are becoming more defined, which means that choosing a specific role to specialize in is of the essence. It's common for people to be overwhelmed by all the options offered by the social media sphere, which is why it's best to begin your research with general terms before getting into non-standard jobs.

The Role of Social Media in Business

Brand Recognition

The objective of any business with a solid marketing plan is to gain brand recognition. The reason for this is simple; consumers are more inclined to purchase from brands they recognize rather than try their luck with a brand they've never heard of before. This is where social media steps in. Brand building before social media was a grueling task that required a considerable and steady amount of funding. Fortunately, nowadays, you don't need to spend tens of thousands of dollars to build a brand. Promoting your business to the public can compel the audience to look at it, even if they aren't exactly looking for it. This is why it's recommended to opt for an interesting profile and cover photos that will provide a strategic position for your social media page.

Conversation and Buzz

One feature that is common to the most successful social media strategies is the buzz created around a brand. If you find your customers or clients talking about your brand and products, you're doing something right. You can easily see this in big brands where endorsements generate considerable amounts of feedback that can drive the sales forward. You can engage with your audience on social media platforms to get them to discuss a specific topic that you've introduced. It's important to make sure that a human is behind the screen and not a robot or someone with a script. People hate it when they feel that a brand they value isn't valuing them enough to engage with them personally.

Telling a Story

A brand with a story to tell always stands out from competitors that don't have one. In theory, a story may not be all that relevant to the quality or appeal of a certain product or service, but it can make a great difference when you factor in marketing and brand recognition. Sharing your brand's message and mission across a social platform is the best way to have your customers relate to you. Depending on what you deem effective as per your marketing technique, a simple story or an elaborate one can be a matter of strategy.

Data Collection from Audience Research

Audience research entails looking for keywords that your audience use, but not just any old keywords! These are usually keywords related to a specific service or product that you offer. Social media makes it easy to gather this kind of information thanks to the analytic tools it grants to businesses. If you're using

Facebook, you can access the insights by clicking on the insight button of a page that you're an admin of. Likewise, Twitter allows you to check the impressions and insights of every tweet.

Customer Service

Social media has inarguably become one of the major players in the customer service industry. Customers no longer want to call on the phone and have to wait until they can finally reach a human. Giving more power to customers through social platforms like Facebook and Twitter enables them to communicate with you more easily, giving you valuable information to work with to resolve a problem, answer queries, or receive feedback. The best thing about it is that it doesn't involve creating a dedicated call center, which is bound to save you a lot of resources. Most brand users will look for ways to connect effortlessly with that brand on social media before anything else. This is why a social media customer service strategy is a must, as it provides convenience to your customers before they choose to bounce to a competitor.

Brand Loyalty

In business, brand loyalty is a vital metric that defines how likely your customers are to continue doing business with you after their first transaction. Fortunately, the people who follow your business on social media are more likely to be loyal to your brand specifically. In simple terms, this means that the ball is in your court. Keeping those loyal customers happy is directly related to how you engage with them after their first purchase. You can employ many strategies with loyal customers to keep them close and engaged with your brand.

Select a Social Media Platform

It's only natural to feel overwhelmed when attempting to select a social media platform for your new business. There are multiple websites, and they each come with their own set of pros and cons, requiring a little research before you begin strategizing.

Facebook

With over 2.6-billion active users, it's hard to go wrong when you choose Facebook as the main platform for your digital marketing. A small business has a lot to benefit from using Facebook, thanks to the wealth of information it has on billions of users. You can set up a business profile with not only links to your website, but also customized ordering pages that make it possible for users to order directly from the business page.

Facebook allows its users to leave reviews on business pages, directly spreading the word-of-mouth that can help attract new customers. The most advantageous feature that Facebook provides to business page owners is a wealth of tools to help you track your customer's preferences and page statistics. One of the downsides of using this platform is that it may require consistently engaging with your fans to keep them satisfied, which may not be the best choice if you don't have the right people for the job.

YouTube

YouTube is the go-to choice for video content with billions of global viewers. There is also the benefit of making money if your videos go viral and gather a lot of hits. You don't necessarily have to pay YouTube to put your content there, but the videos you post should be informative, entertaining, and of impeccable quality. This can be an obstacle for a small business that doesn't have dedicated employees to curate content and create videos. YouTube provides businesses with the right tools to build positive customer sentiment more than any other platform out there. Unlike Facebook, it's hard to track the sales generated from YouTube videos, seeing as the number of views or likes aren't clearly related to sales.

Twitter

Compared to other social media websites, Twitter moves at a quicker pace, suitable for businesses that interact with users more frequently. The platform allows you to publish a lot of posts without looking like you're spamming your followers. Customers that regularly visit Twitter are more inclined to enjoy the privacy that this platform provides, which will help you diversify your clientele and fan base. You might want to keep in mind that Twitter only allows a maximum of 280 characters per tweet, which may not be convenient for businesses that like to tell elaborate or long stories to their customers. The reverse-chronologic nature of posts can make it hard at first to coordinate your message to reach a wider audience, so it's less business-friendly than its algorithm-based counterpart, Facebook.

Instagram

Instagram is where all the fun is these days. When you visit this platform, the first things you see are images and videos, so engaging with customers is often a positive experience thanks to the nature of posts. There is room for endless creativity if you invest enough time into coming up with tailored, engaging, and interesting content. For beginners, it's not as complicated to maneuver through since it doesn't require rigorous research into algorithms like Facebook. Instagram uses hashtags as a metric that can track the conversion ratio. It's worth mentioning that it will take a considerable number of resources and time to produce good content that can help you convert visitors into customers, especially when you take into consideration that you'll only be using pictures and short videos to relay your business's message.

Chapter 4: Build Your Brand

Now that you understand the intricacies of social media platforms and the roles they each play, it's time to learn how you can make use of each one. In this chapter, you will become familiar with some of the best tactics and strategies to build your brand in a meaningful way. So far, the previous chapters have been more on the theoretical side. Starting with this chapter, you will need to have a pen and paper handy to start taking actionable notes!

Follow a Thorough Digital Marketing Strategy

A big part of running a successful business is understanding your own strengths and addressing your shortcomings. Since designing a proper digital marketing strategy will be the foundation of building your brand, you need to make sure it's done right. If you don't want to do this entirely by yourself, you can find a dedicated agency that will bring your brand vision to life. Be as concise as possible regarding how you want your brand to be positioned in the market. Are you building a cool young brand that targets gen Z Tik-Tok fans? Or perhaps yours is a classic brand that is all about elegance and finesse? Regardless, you need your marketing strategy to convey your message and identity in a clear and attractive manner that will grab your target customers' attention. If you still don't have the funds to enlist an expensive marketing agency, you can still put together a decent digital marketing strategy by answering the following questions:

- What is the purpose of your brand?

- Which social media platforms are most relevant to your brand and objectives?

- What are your competitors doing, and how are they doing it?

- What can you change or improve to achieve more brand awareness?

As your brand grows, you need to keep in mind that this won't be enough to sustain your desired success rate. Review and assess your objectives regularly.

Maintain Consistency

Nothing confuses and turns away customers more than a brand that is inconsistent with the image it portrays across different platforms. Everything from colors and fonts to the content you share on your socials must be cohesive. Otherwise, your brand will come across as a poorly thought venture. Even if the quality of your product or service is impeccable, if you don't do a good job of showcasing that digitally, you will have a very slim chance of having any success. The goal here is for the public to recognize your brand even without your logo giving it away. It's worth mentioning that this kind of brand awareness often requires lots of resources (time, money, and efforts) before you can reach it. Nevertheless, this aspiration should give you an excellent sense of direction when establishing your brand on different social media platforms.

Aside from the consistency in your message and tone on social media, you should also be consistent in posting. Your target audience is probably already overwhelmed with information from the myriad of accounts they follow on Facebook, Instagram, or any other platform. If you want to keep them engaged and interested in your brand, it's essential that you post frequently; whatever you do, don't go silent for a prolonged period.

Pursue Meaningful Collaborations

Nowadays, it's rare for a brand to grow and thrive without meaningful collaborations with influencers and other brands. That said, not all collaborations will do the trick; you have to form ones that complement your brand persona and, at the same time, won't undermine the other non-marketing efforts you have been deploying. The best approach is to observe your target audience's behavior on social media. Find out which content creators they resonate with and what kind of posts to respond to the most.

You can also make use of the various data collection features, such as Instagram and Facebook polls, to directly ask about the kind of brands your followers would love to see you collaborate with. Not only will you drive up engagement, but the results will greatly help you when updating your digital marketing strategy. The most important thing to keep in mind when collaborating with public figures and brands is alignment and authenticity. The other party should speak the same language as your brand and share similar values. If not, the backlash could be far heavier than your budding brand can survive.

Enhance Your Customers' Mobile Experience

People now increasingly rely on their mobile devices to check and interact on social media. Scrolling on-the-go has become less of a trend and more of a lifestyle. This is how most people spend their commute and leisure times, so it only makes sense to focus on enhancing your customer's mobile experience if you want to build a strong, positive brand. Your website's mobile interface should be a seamless continuation of your desktop one. There should be little to no difference when it comes to navigation controls, visual quality, loading speed, etc. It might be challenging to get that right on the first attempt with limited funds and resources. With trial and error and a lot of testing, you should be able to reach a level of quality that you'd be proud of.

Be Flexible to Change

One of the main advantages new brands have over old, long-established ones is flexibility, along with ease of pivoting their marketing strategy as per customers' preferences. When building your brand, always look for ways to leverage this valuable asset. This will encourage you to take risks and try new approaches without having to worry about changing course whenever necessary. If you believe that creating a spin-off brand to cater to other demographics would be a good idea based on your research, by all means, give it a go! Split your brand into different sub-brands and follow suit with your social media accounts cross-platforms, then evaluate the effectiveness of this tactic. To mitigate your losses, make sure that you have the right controls in place so you can easily revert to your initial setup if this one didn't work out.

Building your brand is a tedious, comprehensive process. In this chapter, we laid out some marketing fundamentals before delving deeper. In the next chapter, you will learn all about creating quality content, and how it can make a world of difference in how your brand is perceived by the public.

Chapter 5: Create Quality Content

In the previous chapters, we explored the power of social media and its ability to strengthen your brand's image. While advertising and posting on social media platforms is easy, the secret to gaining more attention and standing out from your competitors is posting high-quality, shareable content.

Creating quality content is key to attracting a larger audience and keeping them close to your brand. In fact, the quality of your social media page is so important that it must be prioritized in your content planning. The type of content you post does more than simply attract followers and potential customers. Instead of pumping out lousy advertising rhetoric, social media managers should focus on delivering quality content and creating posts that will generate buzz. Some brands favor quantity over quality, which drives their followers away eventually. It doesn't matter if you post once every two to three days; your objective should be to publish quality content. At the same time, consistency is crucial. Do not bombard your followers with dozens of posts every day; use that time to craft your content plan instead.

Rather than beat around the bush, we will get straight to the point in this chapter and discuss tangible ways to create compelling content that will help you get more followers organically.

Benefits of Creating and Posting High-Quality Content

- **Foster Engagement with Your Audience**: Quality content instantly generates many likes, comments, and shares, which increases user engagement.

- **Drive More Sales:** The type of content you post indirectly affects the number of products you sell.

- **Build Credibility:** Your business will be known for the quality of its content, which will strengthen your followers' trust in your brand.

- **Create a New Brand Image:** If you upload content that follows your brand's color palette, visuals, and values, it will ultimately help reshape your brand's image and give it a new dimension.

Effective Strategies to Create Engaging Content

Now that you know why maintaining content quality on social media is essential, you must learn how to do it. Take a look at a few of these effective content creation strategies to increase engagement, gain more followers, and build a name for yourself.

1. Use Visuals

Since most social media users have an attention span of 3 seconds on average, they are less likely to go through a text-only post. Besides, not everyone likes to read long paragraphs. They will simply scroll past your post, thereby reducing its impact and putting your efforts to waste. To resolve this, use as many images, videos, and graphics, as you can to make your posts self-explanatory, interesting, and visually appealing. If your brand has a dedicated color scheme, add the shades in your posts to create your own identity. A dedicated social media page is visually consistent and has its own identity that makes it unique. Whether it's an Instagram story or a Facebook post, your content will only be consumed if it contains visuals. Hiring a professional designer to achieve visual consistency on your social media pages might be a good idea for you.

2. Post Original and Unique Content

Copied content is extremely off-putting and can backfire. Do not copy or create content that has already been published. You may end up losing a lot of followers, along with your credibility in some cases. Make sure that your content is original and offers novelty. One way of doing this is by understanding your audience and tailoring the content accordingly. Create consumer personas using demographics like gender, age, nationality, level of income, education, etc. Include criteria such as interests, hobbies, and likes or dislikes to get a more in-depth understanding of your audience.

In case you run out of ideas, you can simply shoot behind-the-scenes clips and share them on your pages. This will bring your audience closer to you and allow them to gain an understanding of the people behind the products.

3. Resort to Storytelling

Storytelling is an effective tactic to bring people closer to your brand and relate to its values. Such campaigns can garner instant attention and go viral, as many users will relate to them. Tell stories through your posts. Trigger emotions by sharing personal stories of the brand and team members or shoot a campaign that revolves around a heartfelt tale. Emotions such as joy, happiness, or even sorrow make content stronger and highly relatable. In other words, speak *with* your audience instead of speaking *to* them. This will make your followers feel closer to your brand, which is beneficial for your business in the long run. Avoid co-opting causes and stories that are irrelevant to your brand, as these can easily fail.

4. Interaction is Key

Encourage your audience to interact with your posts by organizing contests and offering rewards, and asking your followers to like, comment, and share your posts. The huge ripple that follows makes the initial investment worthwhile. That's the ultimate goal of social media, namely, to create interaction generated by commenting, liking, and sharing posts. Create your own hashtags and ask your followers to share their personal stories by tagging your brand and using said hashtags. User-generated content leverages engagement and increases your brand's outreach. This will not only foster interaction but also make your content more unique. In parallel, make your content shareable for your followers to spread it to a wider audience. This will help you gain more followers and boost your brand's online presence significantly.

5. Impart Value in Your Content

Informative posts are highly engaging and keep your followers hooked. Say you own a brand that produces cruelty-free makeup products. Your posts can include information related to animal cruelty to educate your followers on the benefits of choosing cruelty-free cosmetics. Throw in a few facts and statistics that you have researched, to make your content more credible. Since these posts are not always entertaining, you must make them visually appealing. Your goal is to compel your followers to pause for a brief moment when scrolling through social media and consume your content.

The best way to float informative posts is by using infographics, which utilize visuals and facts to explain a complex topic in a simple way, thereby making it easier for all kinds of people to appreciate. Infographics also look simple and appealing, which solves the limited attention span dilemma.

6. Follow the Trend and Current Affairs

Trendy topics tend to reach a wider audience, given the traction they generate among users. Several social media platforms also work with algorithms that increase the visibility of posts following trends and the latest news.

Posts related to new trends and current affairs are widely consumed by social media users and largely circulate around platforms. Real-time industry news will also do wonders for your social media image, as your followers will look forward to your posts. When discussing sensitive topics such as racism, feminism, or LGBT rights, think twice as they may trigger negative reactions in your audience. If your brand supports bold values, take that path openly, and follow your beliefs. If possible, start your own trend and spread it across social media pages to gain attention and take valuable credit.

To successfully incorporate content related to current affairs, you must stay on your feet and have a designer churn out a post as soon as any piece of relevant news breaks. The sooner you post, the better engagement and attention you will generate. Add a strong call-to-action in your posts or caption to urge your followers to interact with your content.

7. Use Humor

If you want to keep your social media language light and breezy, employing humor is an ideal choice. Several brands have upped their social media presence by using humor. It isn't always necessary to produce funny images and videos; posting a witty one-liner on Twitter can go a long way. Here are a few examples to understand this scenario. A well-known toilet paper company, Charmin, tweets humorous one-liners with the hashtag "tweetfromtheseat", which has garnered plenty of attention from online users. Another brand that understands the value of humor is the popular cookie company Oreo. They are known for their quirky comebacks and funny visuals on their social media pages.

Irrespective of the time and type of post, wit, puns, and light humor are always well-received by the public. If you manage to make your audience chuckle, they will look forward to your posts every day and become loyal customers.

These seven strategies for creating quality content are absolute winners and will help up your social media game. Mix and match all the tips mentioned above to create a strong, lasting impact. When posting, write your caption with precision, use hashtags, and tag relevant accounts. Post your content when the interaction and engagement seem to be the highest. Research the ideal posting schedule and stick to it. Finally, consider hiring a professional designer to create high-quality content, as they possess a knack for visual elements and will help your social media page look aesthetically appealing. Ultimately, your main goal is to drive consumer action through your content. After all, content is king!

Chapter 6: Craft Your Social Media Strategy

Taking your brand to social media will only yield results if you strategize your moves and create an effective marketing plan. This is especially important if you do not have the luxury of hiring a social media marketer. Since most brands start out with a little budget and a lot of aspirations, getting the marketing right is crucial. Your social media strategy is at the crux of your company's success, as the past 3 to 4 years have shown, given the phenomenal boom in the popularity of social media.

This chapter offers a step-by-step approach to craft an effective social media strategy to benefit your business.

Step 1: Set Your Goals

For effective results, start by establishing your goals as it will give you a clear vision of what you wish to accomplish and push you in the right direction. What do you want your brand to achieve through social media marketing? Is it to create an online presence, attract more customers, gain recognition, stand apart from your competitors, or drive more sales? Unless you set goals from the start, you have no defined destination to reach.

Set SMART Goals

Specific: Your goals should be well-defined and put forward with a clear vision. In other words, shape them into tangible objectives to be able to achieve them easily.

Measurable: Measurable goals inform you of whether your strategies are working or not. They must be quantifiable in numbers.

Attainable: There is little point in setting goals that are hardly achievable. Set your objectives based on the time, budget, and caliber at your disposal. Aiming to get 100,000 followers by the end of the year, although admirable, is a long shot and almost impossible to achieve.

Relevant: Your goals should be in line with your social media strategy. For instance, if you want to create brand awareness, setting objectives to improve customer service can seem irrelevant.

Time-Bound: When it comes to social media marketing, every brand aims to get more followers and increase its reach in as little time as possible. Since social media has the power to fulfill this need, craft your objectives based on a specific, strategic timeline.

The SMART goals approach works each time if applied correctly, which is also true with social media. Establishing goals also helps you narrow down the ideal social media platforms to promote your brand on. As mentioned previously, you must choose no more than two to three social media platforms. An objective crafted using the SMART approach will give you a clear vision and make your social media strategy realizable.

Step 2: Define Your Target Audience

Using social media for marketing purposes involves reaching the right kind of audience to garner their attention and increase your reach. This can only be done by targeting the right user group. Let's look at how to achieve this.

Consider Customer Demographics

Consider your target audience's demographics to define your ideal customer and increase your reach. This includes factors like age, gender, nationality, location, profession, education, level of income, personal interests, etc. Remember that these people are real with real needs and wants; targeting these needs will help shape your social media strategy.

Research Users' Social Media Habits

Once you define your target audience, it is time to dig deeper. Begin by researching user habits across various social media platforms for a better understanding of your followers. Familiarize yourself with their likes, dislikes, favorite platforms, average daily social media screen time, and the way they interact with brands on social media.

You should also consider the type of platform your potential customers use. For instance, you can find people above the age of 35 using Facebook more than the Gen Z population, but don't make assumptions without conducting proper research first.

Create Customer Personas

Upon collecting this data, you can easily define your target audience and create content based on their interests. For example, brands promoting baby products will likely define their target audience as women aged 20 to 40. Similarly, if your company manufactures shaving products, your ideal audience is men within the age group of 17 to 65.

Note that your ideal audience will certainly evolve over time, hence the importance of updating your customer persona periodically.

Step 3: Research the Market

It is always crucial to understand the market, study the available resources, and learn more about your competitors to create a meaningful social media strategy.

Track Vanity Metrics

While most social media platforms provide analytics elements to measure the number of likes, followers, and reach; tracking vanity metrics will help you understand the real value of your social media strategy. Aspects like conversion rates, click-through, and engagement should be focused on. The metrics you research also vary depending on the platform in question, your goals, and your target audience. For instance, if your main objective is to create brand awareness, you should count the number of likes and shares on your Instagram posts; likewise, click-throughs should be measured on LinkedIn to convert leads and drive more traffic. Cost-per-click (or CPC) is another valuable metric used on Facebook. Use free and paid online analytics tools such as Google Analytics and StatCounter to gather relevant data.

Choose a Platform

The content you create should also align with the platform you choose to promote your business on. The ideal platform to market your brand depends on the type of products or services you sell, as well as the message you wish to spread. For example, brands that sell food or clothing items should opt for Instagram, Facebook, or Pinterest, as these platforms support visual content. By contrast, a company specializing in money transfer and currencies will likely favor Twitter and LinkedIn. Of course, this also depends on your target audience and the kind of platform they use. The user personas established earlier will help you make an ideal choice. Tools like Google Analytics help monitor traffic on a website and narrow down searches based on the platforms used by a specific audience. You can then align the search results with your defined target audience.

The Rule of Thirds

While establishing and following one objective is vital, abiding by the rule of thirds will keep your business flowing and your social media game strong. This will not only attract more followers and potential leads but also help to retain your followers and existing customers. With the rule of thirds, you can drive more revenue while boosting your social media presence.

According to this rule:

- A third of your content and posts should be related to your company's values, ideas, thoughts, or trends that revolve around the products and services you endorse. It can also include content promoted by a direct competitor or a similar brand.

- A third of your posts encourage the promotion of your business by uploading content related to your products or services. This will convert your leads into customers and stimulate revenue growth.

- Finally, a third of your content should be dedicated to generating user engagement and bringing your audience closer to your brand.

Just like how individuals hate people who are self-centered, they may despise businesses that are confined and establish boundaries. In this case, collaborating with other brands or revamping your content can help you take your business to another level.

Lastly, learn more about your competitors, the content they post, and the platforms they use. Once you gather this data, dig deeper into your competitors' social media engagement. Learn what works for them and implement the same strategies. By implementing, we mean getting inspired by the approach and not downright content copying. Pay attention to the voice and tone of the content posted, media used, and the content type to adopt the strategies that will work for your brand.

Step 4: Prepare a Content Plan

A content plan is crucial to strengthen your company's social media presence. As you know, content is king; the type of content you post will make or break your brand's online face. While producing quality content is important, the time and manner of posting are just as vital. Follow these steps to design a content plan and stick to it to optimize your brand's online presence.

Focus on Quality Content

Garner your audience's attention by creating relatable and visually appealing content. It should be interactive and shareable. A large part of your online presence and credibility is determined by the quality of your posts.

Design a Visual Identity

When a new user sees your social media page, they must be able to relate to your brand image. A distinguished visual identity is essential to stand out from your competitors and gain recognition. Inexperienced brands often make the mistake of creating multiple visual identities, which ends up confusing their audience. A distinguished visual identity can be developed by using a particular set of colors, respecting a theme, or consistent use of certain visual elements. For example, Dropbox uses a set of simple hand-drawn illustrations that are consistently used across their social media posts. When a user looks at their page, they can instantly recognize the brand, thereby making their visual identity a success. Content brainstorming and storyboarding can help you create a visual identity and follow the process effortlessly. When crafting your content plan, keep your visual identity in mind, as it will make the process simpler, and provide inspiration for the type of content you can post.

Consistency is Key

Even if your content is high quality and has the potential to reach millions of users, you will fail to float your content to a wider audience if you do not post consistently. When it comes to social media marketing, consistency is key.

Schedule your posts and devise a plan for the next two weeks. Since you already have the content plan ready and are clear about the types of posts that will be uploaded, your design team can get to work and prepare them for the upcoming weeks. Once the posts are ready, you can schedule and upload them on channels that offer automatic posting features. One of these scheduling tools is CoSchedule, or alternatively you can use a calendar template based on a spreadsheet model. Input the date and time, upload your posts, and add a compelling caption with relevant hashtags. You can also tag accounts to increase your chances of being featured on popular pages.

Step 5: Consider Different Types of Marketing

Although social media marketing is a defined niche within the advertising and promotional discipline, you can opt for diversification and use different types of marketing to achieve your goals.

Influencer Marketing

Influencer marketing is a new and widely acclaimed promotion strategy used by big and small businesses alike on social media. Brands hire influencers, namely social media celebrities known for their ability to 'influence' their followers. These bloggers often pick a specific topic such as fashion, beauty, makeup, health, fitness, or travel and provide reviews and tips to followers who follow their advice religiously. You can take advantage of these partnerships and hire influencers to promote your products and generate new content. Brands hire micro and mega-influencers on social media to connect with their target audience and increase their follower count organically. While some influencers ask for a hefty fee, the engagement generated makes the investment worthwhile.

Micro-influencing is a growing niche within influencer marketing, where bloggers with 10,000 or fewer followers are hired to promote all sorts of products. Since these influencers have dedicated followers and a wide reach, you can target several potential customers at once without spending a lot of money. Moreover, micro-influencers will often exert great effort to produce creative content to get more such opportunities in the future. In the end, this gives your product a new face and your social media page innovative content to post.

Visual Marketing

Visual marketing is another effective social media strategy as it appeals to every kind of audience internationally. Since most platforms are designed to encourage the posting of visual content, you must take full advantage of their interface. Social media has permeated into every aspect of a person's life, and over 80% of users engage with visual content. Today, more than 74% of digital marketers incorporate visual identities and aesthetic posts as part of their marketing strategy to please their audience.

By harnessing the power of this form of marketing, you can boost interaction and bring your audience closer to your brand. As mentioned above, creating a visual identity and making appealing posts is crucial to attract users and keep them hooked.

Affiliate Marketing

This type of marketing is similar to influencer marketing, where brands hire content creators and influencers to promote their products. The only difference is the payment method. While influencer marketing involves paying a fixed amount to influencers for promoting a product, affiliate marketing pays content creators based on the number of products they sell or the leads they generate. In the latter case, content creators are given a unique affiliate code that is linked to their ID. They create content around the product and offer a code to their followers that must be entered when buying the product on the brand's website.

The content creator must also provide a call-to-action feature for their followers to visit the brand's landing page. When they promote their product and generate leads, brands track cookies to see whether the traffic is generated from the creator's end. They are then paid an amount, usually a commission or percentage, based on the number of sales they were able to generate. Affiliate marketing is beneficial for businesses as it pays only for the number of sales or leads generated.

Step 6: Promote Your Content

Invariably, your content must reach the widest audience possible to increase your brand's visibility. This can be achieved by promoting your content by leveraging various strategies. After all, you cannot expect your content to be promoted by word-of-mouth recommendations and experience success overnight; it will take dedication, time, and effort to make your strategies successful.

Like, Comment, and Interact with Other Brands

You will attract attention and foster engagement if you give it to others in the first place. By liking, commenting, and sharing other brands and influencers' posts, you can expect the same support from others, too. Be creative when writing comments to get more likes and profile visits. As a brand, witty and encouraging comments and replies will do wonders for your social media presence.

Create an Online Community

Platforms such as LinkedIn and Facebook harbor online communities with members who share valuable insights and discuss relevant topics. This is an effective way to reach your target audience and build an organic reach. Even if your social media page has been inactive for a while, these communities help keep your brand's interaction and engagement levels alive.

Online communities in Facebook groups, Reddit discussion forums, and Twitter threads bring together like-minded people who engage in interesting conversations related to a specific topic. At times, businesses put an agenda forward and invite community members to express their thoughts and opinions. Since communication is essential to create engagement and promote any business, creating online communities is a proven method to keep your audience entertained. It also improves customer service, as members are given the freedom to inquire on the brand's approach or respond to a new product launch. To maintain sentiment and passion among your audience, make sure they are heard and that their thoughts are acknowledged.

The Importance of CTAs

As mentioned, effective call-to-action features are key to sharing your content across various platforms on social media. If you create valuable content, give your audience a chance to share it easily. While most platforms offer shareable features on stories, feed, and personal messages, you must provide a powerful CTA for your audience if you want them to visit your landing page and purchase your products (that is, if your ultimate goal is to generate more leads and drive more sales). When it comes to promoting your posts on social media, incorporate CTAs in a natural way. They shouldn't feel forced or overly promotional.

Unique, genuine, and creative CTAs go a long way, and your content will be shared beyond expectations. For example, organizing contests, asking questions, holding quizzes, and offering free resources are some ways you can seamlessly incorporate CTAs in your content.

Run Ads on Social Media

Most social media platforms offer promotional features and the ability to run ads to reach your target audience. As such, dedicate a portion of your marketing budget to promote your content on social media with paid ads. Platforms such as Instagram and Facebook offer paid promotions at a specific daily rate based on the number of users you wish to reach. You can also specify the type of audience you want to reach by entering demographic details and narrowing your search. This helps you get more organic followers. The algorithm of these paid ads target users who are interested in similar styles and language, thereby encouraging them to follow your page. Again, your content must be powerful and appealing to users to gain more followers and fulfill your marketing objectives.

These steps will guarantee that your brand is promoted to the widest possible audience and gets the online visibility it needs. By paying attention to the details, you won't need to hire a social media specialist to improve your follower count, build your brand's image, and drive more sales.

Most importantly, stick to your values and the message you wish to deliver, as it will affect your brand's credibility. At times, it may just take one viral post to turn your social media page and strategy into an overnight success. Even if your post goes viral, you may not necessarily gain a lot of followers if your virtual identity doesn't seem promising. This is when an effective, thought-out social media strategy will come to your rescue and allow you to enjoy the attention your brand deserves.

Chapter 7: Enhance Your Reach and Engagement

We have come to one of the most frequently asked questions, especially since it doesn't have a straightforward answer: How do you enhance your brand's reach and foster engagement on social media? This is the question self-starters and multi-billion-dollar brands alike spend hours of their "screen-time" attempting to decipher. Although working out the algorithm is a complicated matter, it's definitely doable. By the end of this chapter, you should have a clear understanding of how to manipulate the algorithm to your favor and leverage it to make the most out of your social platforms. So, let's get right to it!

What Exactly Are Algorithms?

Before we delve into how you can win over social media algorithms, it's important to understand what they are in the first place. The purpose of algorithms is to filter the posts on these platforms according to their relevance to users. Now, to grow your brand on social media, you must find ways to create the sort of content that appeals to the algorithm of different networks. That way, your posts will yield more engagement and reach even more users. Continue reading for simple strategies that'll help you do just that.

Keep the Conversation Going

Social media algorithms take notice of accounts that know how to keep their followers engaged. Frequent surveys and invitations to followers to share their opinions have proven their success in keeping the conversation going between brands and their followers. The concept of social media is to connect people, so it only makes sense that this is the key to expanding your brand's reach. Study your target audience's online behaviors, find out what accounts they follow, as well as what posts they like and share with their friends and followers. This will give you an idea of the conversations that will resonate with them and keep them interested. Given the sheer volume of daily posts on all social platforms, make it a point to bring something new to the table. It doesn't have to be an entirely never-seen-before concept, but it has to look like you made an effort to think about your content before posting. If there's anything social media users despise, its monotony and lack of creativity.

Figure Out How to Use Hashtags

Hashtags group similar content together to make it easier for interested users to find the posts they would enjoy. Too many, and your posts come across as annoying; too few, and they're completely useless. Finding the right number of relevant hashtags to use in your captions can be challenging. According to social media experts, the ideal number of hashtags per post varies from platform to platform. For Facebook and Twitter, 1 to

2 hashtags are enough to get your brand attention. Instagram, on the other hand, encourages users to use up to 30 hashtags per post. Nevertheless, it's not only a matter of quantity; choosing the right hashtags for each post will make your brand more visible and accessible to new users. While trial and error can help you identify the best-performing hashtags, it can be time consuming and not as accurate as you'd expect. Using a social media analytics tool can speed up the process and provide you with more reliable data. Within seconds, you'll be able to see the most popular hashtags and the ones with the longest lifespan.

The next step is to cross-check this information with your target audience and make sure that they will indeed find those hashtags interesting. After that, you will need to evaluate the performance of your hashtags to assess whether your strategy is paying off. Using the same analytics tool, you can find out which hashtags are fostering the most engagement. Once you have a good grip on how hashtags work, and after having incorporated trending ones into your content, you'll want to go a step further and create your very own branded hashtag. Tracking the performance of your branded hashtag will give you a foolproof answer when it comes to how much your brand is being seen on social media. Note that to reap the rewards of a branded hashtag, it's important to make sure it stays consistent with the unique brand image you're trying to put across.

Post Different Types of Content

To maximize your reach, you have to experiment with different types of content. The best performing accounts on social media are those that post a combination of text content, still images, memes, and GIFs, with a special focus on videos. In case you didn't already know, videos are one of, if not the most engaging, type of content across all platforms. A well-executed video uploaded directly onto your feed (rather than a link) will encourage your followers to share it multiple times.

To take it even a step further, try making videos around a buzz-worthy piece of news that everyone is talking about. Your social media accounts grant you the opportunity to weigh in on current events and showcase your brand's involvement in smart and subtle ways. Don't be tone deaf and shamelessly plug your products and services when the topic may be a sensitive one. As a rule, you should maintain a good balance between your promotional and informative posts so as not to come across as pushy or opportunistic.

Go Live At Least Once A Week

The live features on Instagram and Facebook can help increase the engagement of your existing followers and attract new ones. Furthermore, they add the human element to your brand that today's users are mostly drawn to. You don't necessarily need to conduct a scripted live session. That said, it's best to have structure to keep your audience hooked and compel them to join in on the conversation. Build the hype for your weekly live sessions by posting teasers about your next guest and urge your followers to get ready with their questions. You can also hold a monthly giveaway contest under a dedicated hashtag to promote your live sessions beyond your follower base.

Schedule Your Posts Wisely

Generally, the more frequently you post, the higher your chance of increasing your brand's reach and follower count. Since you probably have other tasks to attend to, you need to find a smart way to schedule your posts for maximum effectiveness. Using a scheduling tool, you can easily figure out the peak times when your followers are online and most active. As for the frequency of posting, twice a day is considered adequate for most platforms. Seasoned social media marketers recommend creating bulk content on a weekly basis, so you will always have fresh material ready to post. The scheduling tool will allow you to upload your content as you see fit. Of course, you still need to respond to your followers in a timely manner, which brings us to our next point.

Respond to Your Followers

Replying to every comment and direct message can be daunting, especially since a good chunk will be spam, but it's well worth your time and efforts. Given the fierce competition, responsiveness is a key differentiator between a brand that genuinely cares about its customers and another whose sole motivation is profits. Dedicate at least one hour daily of your social media activities to answering your followers' queries. Analyzing the kinds of questions and comments you receive will open your eyes to the enhancements you need to make your social media pages more appealing to your target audience.

Try to limit automated replies, especially if your followers are expressing their frustration over shipping issues or product quality. In fact, in such cases, not only should you reach out and try to solve your customers' issues but take it as an opportunity to showcase your stellar customer service and offer compensation whenever your budget allows.

Ask for What You Want, Point-Blank

There is absolutely no shame in asking social media users to follow your accounts and share your content. Keep your call-to-action visible and highlight it for optimum results. Think of your social media handles as your signature. In your emails, business cards, and throughout the pages of your website - post your social media links, compelling users to follow, subscribe, and share.

Growing your follower base on social media requires patience and time if you want to make it happen authentically and organically. The tactics mentioned in this chapter will help you throughout this process and remind you what needs to be done at every stage. In the next pages, you will get to explore different social media marketing tools and learn how each one can help you grow a successful, appealing brand.

Chapter 8: Social Media Marketing Tools

Social media marketing operates on simple principles that focus on driving traffic and maximizing the reach of posts. As social media algorithms develop into more complex forms, analyzing all this data can prove difficult without using analytic software and marketing tools. Troubleshooting a problem that is negatively affecting your entire social media strategy can take time if you don't leverage the power of dedicated software. Delivering great content is not done by mentioning a lot of names or writing templates; it takes time, resources, and the right tools to craft it properly and make an impact.

Biteable

Content specifically created for social media pages is an integral part of your marketing strategy. The impact of visual content is not new to marketers. According to Twitter, visual content fosters triple the engagement compared to its textual counterpart. Whether it's on Twitter or Facebook, you need to make sure your content is visual, more often than not. This is where Biteable comes into play. By using Biteable, you don't need to hire a team of graphic designers or animators to produce shareable content on social media. This web-based tool has a fair share of free templates, footage, background music, and animation. As such, no need to learn how to operate studio equipment because Biteable makes the process streamlined and user-friendly.

Buffer

Buffer made a name for itself as one of the best scheduling tools for Twitter. It didn't take long for its success to extend to other social media platforms such as Google, LinkedIn, and Pinterest, among others. Buffer has an extension of its own that makes it easy to drag and drop the content to your queue and then share it. In case you post a lot of links, you'll find convenience with the synchronization features it offers with Bitly. If you choose, you can either upload your own media or drag them from the web into the schedule. Your content's performance can also be tracked directly from the app, giving you a comprehensive and detailed overview. If you'd like to consolidate your interactions, Buffer will help you reply to the posts from inside the software instead of having to switch between your platform of choice and the app.

Buzzsumo

The first step in any marketing strategy is researching your competitors. When building a strategy from the ground up, you'll be dooming your business before you start if you don't know what your competitors are doing and how they're doing it. Research tools are popular for this very reason, and Buzzsumo is one of the best tools among those. It will help you see how your content is faring against competition and who exactly is helping it be shared. Managing a long streak of creating high-quality content is harder than you may think; sometimes, you'll be doing great for a good while, and at other times you'll feel like you have no clue what you're doing. Research tools will boost your odds for success because you'll have a foundation to depend on for your content.

Buzzsumo is great for finding the right content that you can share on social platforms since you'll be able to see what's being shared the most at any given time. It will also provide you with a reliable database of influencers who cover the same topics you're interested in. If you're waiting for certain keywords, links, or names to come up, you can set up alerts to receive them once they appear on the social platform. Take the time to track your competitor's progress and focus on analyzing their content accordingly. Once you have a list of the top keywords that your target audience is interested in, research them with Buzzsumo to find the most suitable topics you should share and post about.

MeetEdgar

If you're looking to create and schedule content consistently, you'll want a content manager by your side to get the job done.

The challenge is that you may not have the budget to get one, or perhaps you're a one-person-band; this is where MeetEdgar can help you out. As a social media management software, MeetEdgar will take care of sharing and re-sharing your content, tweaking your social traffic to meet the target. It focuses on automated actions that have reliable and tangible effects on traffic. You'll have no issues setting it up on Facebook, Twitter, and LinkedIn. Creating content and forgetting about it is a big mistake, so using MeetEdgar will make sure that your social channels are populated with your content, increasing your traffic while engaging with your audience. The scheduling is quite elaborate, as it allows you to combine different types of content based on their category (text, still images, short clips).

Hootsuite

If you operate on multiple social media platforms, nothing can be more useful than a single dashboard that groups all the command controls. Rather than switching back and forth between social media accounts, you can sign up on Hootsuite for free. The best thing about this tool is that it's designed to synchronize collaborations across social media managers and their teams, not to mention the content approval process. Aside from placing social activity in a single trackable interface, it allows you to delegate tasks to team members and schedule regular updates. From community-based platforms like Reddit and Tumblr, to social ones like Facebook and YouTube, a digital marketer has all they need to keep a close eye on the performance and analytics of their brand with Hootsuite.

Mention

As intuitive as its name sounds, Mention is a very versatile social listening tool that allows you to monitor any mention of your brand, products, services, and even your competitor's mentions through real-time metrics. The good news is that Mention is well-integrated and enables you to synchronize with different social platforms, helping you respond to comments and mentions directly within the app. It's also often used to find influencers suitable for various campaigns since it specifically targets mentions.

Zapier

The newest social media marketing tools are noticeably inclined towards automation, which is why Zapier excels at what it does. The process is quite simple; you set up the rules that you want your marketing to follow, and it will execute them efficiently. These rules can trigger an action once the system notices something. For example, you can have Zapier create a dedicated doc file with the notification information once someone mentions your brand. This will help alleviate time-consuming tasks and streamline the process to only focus on what matters to your brand's growth. It's worth mentioning that Zapier is a relatively complex tool that will require you to spend time learning its ins and outs, so it's more geared towards businesses that are highly focused on automation.

AdEspresso

With an attention-driving name such as this, AdEspresso is one of the biggest names in A/B testing. It allows you to experiment with your ads, no matter how complex they are. Many digital marketers fall into the trap of guessing the significance and influence of their ads, albeit understandably at times, but it should never be the norm. AdEspresso makes the results of your ads tangible thanks to its quick real-time analysis of the major social platforms ads like Facebook, Google, and Instagram. You can launch several ads to various platforms from the same dashboard, in addition to monitoring how they fare individually. You can take the time to test different media, copies, ads, and titles to see which combination best suits your expectations. All the important metrics that you'll need to optimize the ad and create it can be found in a customizable, user-friendly dashboard.

Bitly

The problem with lengthy URLs is that they are tricky, hard to remember, and sometimes can be difficult to share. Shortening URLs is a quick and super convenient process in many situations. Short URLs don't only look better, but they are much easier to share around and drive more leads to your website. Bitly is an effective tool for shortening long, confusing URLs to make them easier to remember and more convenient to share. Bitly doesn't only get the job done effortlessly, but it also comes with a simple interface and plenty of advantages that marketers can leverage to acquire all the analytics that can make or break their strategies.

Rebrandly

Lastly, like Bitly, Rebrandly is another famous one in the field that does a great job of shortening your URLs and creating custom or branded URLs. The link you share online is correlated to your reputation, so sharing random links that look like spam may drive potential customers away from clicking on the link. You can use custom links to enhance brand awareness and increase the link's trust that algorithms set. You'll find some useful additional features like traffic routing and QR code integration to further optimize your links.

Chapter 9: Monitor and Measure Success

Imagine spending a sizable budget on social media marketing without being able to track how successful your campaign is. It's important not to get lost drifting through numerous metrics that you don't understand. Monitoring and measuring your performance is essential to any social media marketer or business owner, which is why you should take it to the next level once you have your tools and strategies set to go. This final chapter explores how you can keep track of your social media marketing success.

The Two Categories of Social Media Measurement

Before you begin measuring your metrics and parameters, it's important to know the context in which you're operating. There are two main types of social media measurement, namely, ongoing monitoring and campaign-focused monitoring.

• On-Going Analytics

To keep a close ear to the pulse of your campaign, on-going analytics are crucial for monitoring the tone of the conversations about your brand. It's automated by most social media platforms and tools, making it easy to track your brand's progress every step of the way.

• Campaign-Based Analytics

The impact of your marketing strategies isn't exactly measured by on-going analytics but rather campaign-focused metrics. The influence of a strategy can vary from one campaign to another, since its goals are different most of the time (brand building, driving engagement, lead conversion, and such).

Follower Growth

Follower growth is an important metric that lets you know how successful your social media campaign and presence are. The total number of followers and likes are directly related to people's interest in your brand. Naturally, your content will be the motor in the increase of your followers and tracking it is imperative for the improvement of your campaigns.

• Facebook

You can get a broad and detailed analysis of your page likes by visiting the Insights section on your Facebook page. There, you will see the total number of likes, in addition to a detailed analysis of losses and gains within a specific timeframe. This will help you monitor how your audience reacts to each of your posts, not to mention that you'll be able to figure out the right time to post your content.

• Twitter

What's handy on Twitter is being able to view trends and statistics relevant to your own followers. Click on Twitter Analytics and choose your profile from the top, then select analytics from the menu. You'll find a row of essential parameters that summarize a 28-day period. Within this, you can see a percentage analysis of your tweets, impressions, profile visits, mentions, and follower gain/loss. It's important to visit this page regularly if your campaign involves marketing on Twitter.

Knowing the Right Time to Engage

If you want to track how well your campaign is doing, knowing when to post and when to monitor is key. Your marketing strategy should be specifically tailored to release content at the right time, and it's not exclusively about the time of the day. In fact, your audience will be most active on certain days of the week, holidays, during on-going trends, and other strategic timings that give you a suitable window to post new content and interact with them.

• Facebook

On Facebook, you can easily find your followers' daily activity over a period of 7 days, and you can customize the overview to see which individual days enjoy the highest engagement rates. You can get additional specs and monitor how engagements are affected hour by hour in real-time. To check these metrics, go to your Insights section, click posts, and choose 'when your fans are online.' Select any day of the week to view the engagement rates.

• Twitter

When you compare Twitter to Facebook, you'll find that the platform doesn't provide many in-depth tools to measure user engagement, such as engagement statistics to specific hours of the day. However, you can still check the engagement rates on a day-by-day basis. By clicking on the tweets tab, you'll see a graph representing the rises and falls of engagement over the last month.

Likes and Reactions for Specific Posts

This is a core digital marketing strategy you need to be aware of, to set your expectations and properly strategize the nature of your content. Your audience will react to the content you post, and fortunately, platforms like Facebook have recently introduced reactions to gauge how the audience feels about a certain publication. This is a straightforward metric that can help you analyze the topics your audience is most interested in. If you notice the audience is more reluctant to view the content, it may be your cue to avoid a certain topic, language, or style. You may find that certain types of content resonate more through different channels to a different audience, so experimenting around with this should prove useful.

• Facebook

Facebook is quite popular for its system that provides in-depth analytics with its recently developed reaction style. It makes it easy to know whether your audience likes, loves, dislikes, or is angry about the content you've posted or shared. You should be able to know every single post's general reaction from the public with just a few clicks. These metrics are available under the "Insights" tab. If you want a more conclusive view, you'll find the total reactions per post, but you can also see a specific view of each type of reaction through the post link.

• Twitter

Even though Twitter's engagement metrics aren't as comprehensive as Facebook, it provides a similar setup that displays your tweets chronologically. You can view your most engaging Tweets by selecting 'Top Tweets.' The engagement column has information that contains more 'noise' than Facebook; it can sometimes confuse you during analysis, especially when you take into account that any interaction with the tweet in question, from comments to retweets, is considered a measurable metric. Head to the 'Likes' graph to see how many likes you're averaging per day, which is useful data that you can build on to optimize your campaign.

Measure Content Shareability

If you want your content to become a hot topic of conversation, it's about time to look into the elements that make it shareable. As a target, it's easier to achieve a higher like count than shares, but that route is the easy one. Shares are the best way to get your content in front of every type of audience. People may like certain content, but they may not be sure enough that others would as well. Shares are concrete proof that users value the content, in addition to recommending that others view it, too. Shared content is often found relevant and has a strong emotional value that nudges the audience into sharing it, giving you an even wider reach. Finding the number of shares on Facebook or retweets on Twitter can be done easily from the post's link.

Referral Traffic

Referral traffic isn't measured using tools provided to you by the platform and may require the use of acquisition data. The traffic you get from a social media platform directly to your website is called referral traffic. Using this data can help you assess whether certain channels aren't performing as well as you've expected, requiring you to add extra calls to action and improved campaign features. To get your hands-on referral traffic data, use Google Analytics and access acquisition from the site's menu. It should provide you with an overview of the traffic you're getting from each social network you're operating on. You can also get more specific information by accessing the 'Network Referrals' tab to view the session counts and the number of pages visited.

Determine Reach

Social media success might seem like a numbers game, but in reality, it goes much deeper than that. Determining your page's reach is essential to gauge the effectiveness of your marketing strategy, plan your next move, and discover any adjustments your pages might need. Reach metrics essentially show the number of people your pages managed to reach. These numbers, however, do not differentiate between your target audience and users outside your audience. To improve the visibility of your page, especially if the numbers indicate reach from external users, you need to generate more engaging, interesting, and shareable content. This way, you will make sure that your content attracts more attention. Avoid getting tunnel-vision when you're targeting a high reach count since it can affect you negatively if you pursue the wrong campaign. Researching the content and anticipating the audience's reaction to it before broadcasting it to even more people is crucial to avoid any mishaps that often accompany mediocre content. Ultimately, keep in mind that impressions are different from reach; the latter is calculated for unique visitors and not the number of times it shows up.

Conclusion

It's time to wrap up this journey of how you can use social media marketing to grow your brand. Throughout his book, we covered various topics to provide you with a practical guide that would remain relevant during the different phases of your brand's life.

In the opening chapter, we discussed the real power of social media and its impact on today's business. You should now have a solid understanding of how social media unfolded organically to make information more accessible for everyone. Whether it became what it is today intentionally or not, the "humanification" of business came in strong in the last few years, further strengthening the power and reach of social media.

Chapter 2 was a dissection of the most popular social media platforms including Facebook, Instagram, Snapchat, Reddit, and everything in between. We highlighted the potential of each platform and offered valuable tips on how to evaluate them to determine the right mix for your brand based on your aspirations and the type of content you want to create.

Chapter 3 opened your eyes to the role social media and content marketing play in making or breaking a brand. This concluded the theoretical section of the book and prepared you for the remaining chapters that laid out applicable strategies and tactics to tackle the world of social media.

Starting with Chapter 4, we went through some tried and tested approaches to give you a head start in the vast social media realm. You got to learn firsthand the importance of a well laid-out digital marketing strategy to act as a foundation for your efforts across the different platforms. By the end, we stressed the fact that staying nimble and quick on your feet is bound to serve you well on your way to building your brand successfully.

Chapter 5 was entirely dedicated to quality content, given its impact on engagement, sales volume, and your brand image. We mentioned several strategies that can help you create high-quality and effective posts to keep your followers engaged and eager to see more of your captivating content.

Chapter 6 was indeed a heavy one. It was designed as a step-by-step guide on how you can craft your own social media strategy with minimal help from industry experts, starting from setting your goals and defining your target audience, to researching the market and preparing a content plan. Finally, we displayed the different types of marketing you can use to achieve your goals, carrying you well into the final stage of promoting your content and maximizing the visibility of your brand.

We then moved to Chapter 7, where it was all about maneuvering the algorithm of social media platforms and making them work in your favor. By now, it's safe to say that you have some strategies at your disposal that you can rely on to enhance your reach and engagement on social media.

In Chapter 8, we introduced some leading social media marketing tools to help you manage your social accounts in a smarter, more efficient manner.

Lastly, we concluded this book by discussing the importance of continually evaluating your marketing strategies to measure their efficacy and make any necessary changes to stay on top of your game.

Now that this ride has come to an end, we urge you to apply everything you learned in this book. We can't promise it will be easy; you will stumble and fumble before you eventually find your voice and make a name for yourself on social media. That's the exciting thing about the virtual world: nothing is set in stone. If your initial plans fall through, change your course of action, and try different strategies. Before you know it, you will succeed at making your brand the next online sensation!

Printed in the USA
CPSIA information can be obtained
at www.ICGtesting.com
LVHW012151141123
763978LV00030B/620